Fun for Kids
Englisch mit Witzen

Von Karen Richardson
Mit Zeichnungen von Hans-Jürgen Feldhaus

Langenscheidt

Berlin · München · Wien · Zürich
London · Madrid · New York · Warschau

www.langenscheidt.de

Umschlaggestaltung: init.büro für gestaltung, Bielefeld

Umwelthinweis: gedruckt auf chlorfrei gebleichtem Papier

© 2010 by Langenscheidt KG, Berlin und München
Satz: Franzis print & media GmbH, München

Druck: CS-Druck CornelsenStürtz GmbH & Co. KG, Berlin
Printed in Germany

ISBN 978-3-468-20750-1

Inhalt

Animal Jokes

What time is it when an elephant sits on the fence?

Time to get a new fence!

Was für eine Uhrzeit ist es, wenn ein Elefant
auf dem Zaun sitzt?
Zeit, einen neuen Zaun zu kaufen!

When does a dog say "moo"?

When it is learning a new language!

Two frogs are sitting by a pond. Suddenly it starts raining. One frog says to the other: "Quick! Let's jump into the water, or we'll get wet!"

Zwei Frösche sitzen an einem Teich. Plötzlich beginnt es zu regnen. Da sagt der eine Frosch zum anderen: "Schnell, lass uns ins Wasser springen, sonst werden wir nass!"

What's a slug?

A homeless snail!

Was ist eine Nacktschnecke?
Eine obdachlose Schnecke!

Two mice are looking out of the window.
They see a bat flying.
Says one mouse to the other: "Look! An angel!"

"Schau mal, ein Engel!"
Sagt die eine Maus zur anderen:
Sie sehen eine Fledermaus vorbeifliegen.
Zwei Mäuse schauen aus dem Fenster.

Why do elephants not ride bicycles?

**Because they don't have thumbs
to ring the bell!**

What's the worst thing about being an octopus?

Washing your hands before dinner.

Was ist das Schlimmste, wenn man eine Krake ist?
Das Händewaschen vor dem Essen!

12

Why do fish swim in salt water?

Because pepper makes them sneeze!

Warum schwimmen Fische in Salzwasser?
Weil sie von Pfeffer niesen müssen!

What's big and grey and has 16 (sixteen) wheels?

An elephant on roller-blades!

What did the spider do on the computer?

She made a website!

(Das englische Wort für Spinnennetz ist „spider's web".)
Sie hat eine Website gemacht!
Was hat die Spinne am Computer gemacht?

15

What did the boy octopus say to the girl octopus?

I wanna hold your hand, hand, hand, hand, hand, hand, hand, hand!

Was sagte der Tintenfischjunge
zu dem Tintenfischmädchen?
Ich möchte deine Hand, Hand, Hand,
Hand, Hand, Hand, Hand, Hand halten!

Doctor Jokes

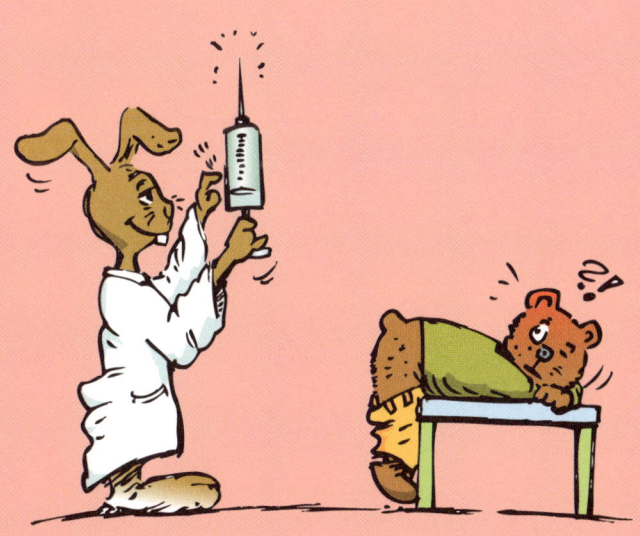

Doktor, Doktor, ich habe gerade ein Schaf verschluckt!
Wie fühlen Sie sich?
Sehr mäh-mäh-ßig!
(„Englischsprachige" Schafe machen das Tiergeräusch
„ba-a-a-a" und nicht „mäh" wie deutsche Schafe!)

Doktor, Doktor, ich glaube, ich bin unsichtbar.
Wer hat das eben gesagt?

Doktor, Doktor, alle denken, ich sei eine Lügnerin.
Das glaube ich Ihnen nicht!

What do you call a doctor with eight arms?

A doctopus.

Einen Doktopus.

Wie nennt man einen Arzt mit acht Armen?

Doctor, doctor, I think I'm a dog!

Please sit down on this chair and tell me about it.

I can't, I'm not allowed on the chairs!

Doktor, Doktor, ich glaube, ich bin ein Hund!

Nehmen Sie bitte auf diesem Stuhl Platz und erzählen Sie mir davon.

Geht nicht – ich darf nicht auf Stühle!

23

Doktor, Doktor, ich glaube, ich brauche eine Brille!
Das glaube ich auch, mein Herr.
Dies ist ein »Fish and Chip Shop«!

Doktor, Doktor, ich habe mein Gedächtnis verloren!
Wann haben Sie es verloren?
Wann habe ich was verloren?

Language Jokes

What do you find on a small beach?

Microwaves!

Was findest du an einem kleinen Strand?
Mikrowellen!
(In diesem Witz steckt ein Wortspiel: Die Vorsilbe „micro-" kommt
ursprünglich aus dem Griechischen und bedeutet so viel wie „sehr klein"!)

What kind of fast food do frogs like to eat?

French flies!

Französische Fliegen!

Was für eine Art von Fastfood essen Frösche gerne?

Where do cows go on Saturday night?

To the moo-vies!

(Das englische Wort für Kino wird wie „Muuh-wiehs" ausgesprochen.)
Ins Kino!
Wohin gehen Kühe am Samstagabend?

30

What kind of bird can write?

A "pen-guin"!

What do you call a computer superhero?

A screensaver!

(In diesem Witz steckt ein Wortspiel: Wörtlich übersetzt heißt
"screensaver" „Bildschirm-Retter".)
Einen Bildschirmschoner!
Wie nennt man einen Computer-Superhelden?

What kind of horse can swim underwater?

A sea horse!

Welches Pferd kann unter Wasser schwimmen?
Ein Seepferdchen!

What do you call an Eskimo cow?

An Eskimoo!

Wie nennt man eine Eskimo-Kuh?
Eine Eskimuh!

What do you get if you put your MP3 player in the fridge?

Cool music!

Which Dutch city do hamsters come from?

Hamsterdam!

(In diesem Witz steckt ein Wortspiel: Die Hauptstadt der Niederlande heißt Amsterdam.)
Hamsterdam!
Aus welcher holländischen Stadt stammen Hamster?

Excuse me, do you speak English?

Yes, I do.

No, I don't. I speak Penguish.

Mädchen: Entschuldigen Sie, sprechen Sie Englisch?
Hund: Ja, das tue ich.
Pinguin: Nein, das tue ich nicht. Ich spreche Pinguinisch.

37

What kind of car does Mickey Mouse's girlfriend drive?

A Minnie!

Einen „Minnie"!

Was für ein Auto fährt die Freundin von Micky Maus?

Winter Jokes

What do snowmen eat for breakfast?

Snowflakes!

Schneeflocken!

Was essen Schneemänner zum Frühstück?

What does Santa Claus have after he has delivered all the Christmas presents?

A Santa pause!

Was macht der Weihnachtsmann, nachdem er alle Weih-
nachtsgeschenke abgeliefert hat? Eine Santa Pause!
(In diesem Witz steckt ein Wortspiel: „Santa Pause" reimt sich im
Englischen auf „Santa Claus!")

What does the snowman say to the snow-woman?

Marry me or I'll sit in the sun!

Was sagt der Schneemann zur Schneefrau?
Heirate mich oder ich setze mich in die Sonne!

42

What do monkeys sing at Christmas?

Jungle bells, jungle bells, jungle all the way!

Was singen Affen an Weihnachten?
Dschungel-Glocken, Dschungel-Glocken, Dschungel auf dem ganzen Weg!

How do you know if there's a snowman in your bed?

You wake up wet!

Why do polar bears have fur coats?

Because they'd look stupid in anoraks!

Warum tragen Eisbären einen Pelz?
Weil sie in Anoraks ganz schön blöd aussähen!

How does a cow say Merry Christmas?

Mooey Christmas!

Muuuh! Christmas!
Wie sagt eine Kuh frohe Weihnachten?

Who brings Christmas presents to baby sharks?

Santa Jaws!

Where do snowmen go to dance?

To a snowball!

Kennst du diesen Ozean, Toby?
Nein, nicht persönlich ...

Why did the teacher wear sunglasses?

Because his students were so bright!

Warum trug der Lehrer eine Sonnenbrille?
Weil seine Schüler so helle waren!

What has 40 feet and sings?

A school choir!

What do you get if you cross a vampire and a teacher?

Lots of blood tests!

54

Why did Mickey Mouse go into space?

Because
he wanted
to find Pluto.

Warum flog Mickymaus in den Weltraum?
Weil er Pluto finden wollte.

What are two things you cannot have for breakfast?

Lunch and dinner.

Welche zwei Sachen kannst du nicht zum Frühstück haben?
Mittagessen und Abendessen.

What is green, hairy and wears sunglasses?

A gooseberry on holiday!

Was ist grün, haarig und trägt eine Sonnenbrille?
Eine Stachelbeere im Urlaub!

Why did the silly boy stand on his head?

Because his feet were tired!

Warum stand der dumme Junge auf dem Kopf?
Weil seine Füße müde waren!

What did the big chimney say to the little chimney?

You're too young to smoke!

Was sagte der große Schornstein zu dem kleinen?
Du bist noch zu jung zum Rauchen!

What's red and always goes up and down?

A strawberry in a lift.

Was ist rot und fährt immer auf und ab?
Eine Erdbeere in einem Aufzug!

What runs and runs but hasn't got any feet?

Water!

What should you do if you hate cheese with holes?

Eat the cheese and leave the holes on your plate!

Was solltest du tun, wenn du Käse mit Löchern hasst?
Iss den Käse und lass die Löcher auf dem Teller liegen!

What turns around and around all the time but never gets dizzy?

The Earth!

Who reads and lives in an apple?

A bookworm!

Monster & Witch Jokes

What do sea monsters eat?

Fish and ships!

Was essen Meeresungeheuer?
„Fish and ships" (Fisch und Schiffe)!

Why did the monster take ten months to finish a book?

Because he wasn't very hungry.

Warum brauchte das Monster zehn Monate, um mit dem
Buch fertig zu werden?
Weil es keinen richtigen Appetit hatte!

Why did the witch go to an astrologer?

She wanted to know her horror-scope!

Warum ging die Hexe zu einem Astrologen?
Sie wollte ihr Horror-skop wissen!
(„Horror-scope" ist ein Wortspiel, denn „horoscope" bedeutet Horoskop.)

What do vampires have at eleven o'clock every day?

A coffin break!

(In diesem Witz steckt ein Wortspiel: Die englischen Wörter „coffin" (Sarg)
und „coffee" (Kaffee) hören sich sehr ähnlich an.)
Eine Sarg-Pause!
Was machen Vampire jeden Tag um 11 Uhr?

Why do skeletons drink a lot of milk?

Because it's good for the bones!

Who lives in a sandcastle?

A sand witch!

("Sand witch" klingt im Englischen fast genauso wie das „sandwich".)
Eine Sandhexe!
Wer lebt in einer Sandburg?

73

What kind of dog does Dracula have?

A bloodhound!

Why was the Egyptian boy confused?

Because his daddy was a mummy!

What has six legs and flies?

A witch and her cat on a flying broomstick!

Was hat sechs Beine und fliegt?
Eine Hexe und ihre Katze auf einem fliegenden Besenstiel!

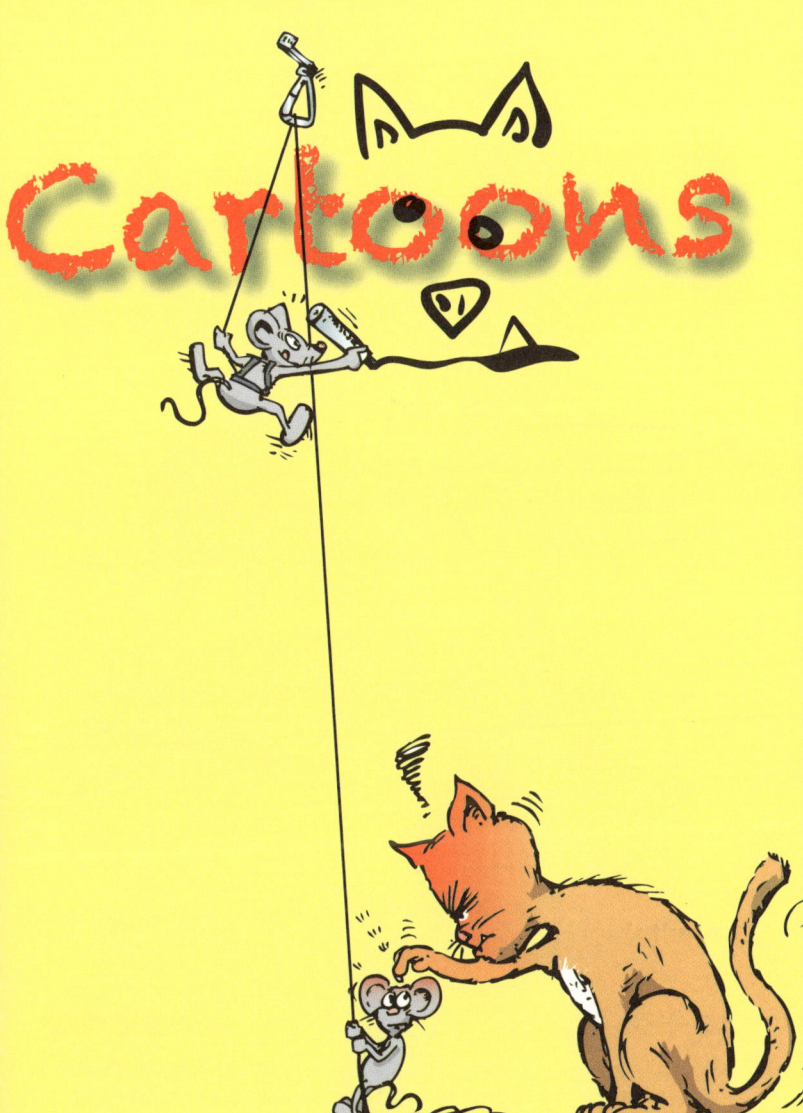

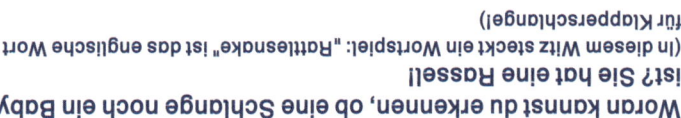

Mein Hund hat keine Nase.
Wie riecht er dann?
Furchtbar!

Hey, bist du krank?
Nein, es geht mir gut. Warum fragst du?
Weil du so grün aussiehst ...

Wie viel Uhr ist es?
Es ist Zeit, dass du gehst!

81

What are you thankful for on Thanksgiving?

I am thankful that
I'm not a turkey.

Wofür bist du dankbar am Erntedanktag?
Ich bin dankbar, dass ich kein Truthahn bin.

83

Herr Ober, was macht die Fliege in meiner Buchstaben-
suppe?
Ich glaube, sie versucht Lesen zu lernen!

Was ist schlimmer, als einen Wurm in seinem Apfel zu finden?
Einen halben Wurm in seinem Apfel zu finden!

86

What does the moth mum tell the moth child at lunchtime?

> FIRST you eat the old socks and THEN you'll get the yummy bikini!

Was sagt die Mottenmama beim Mittagessen zum Mottenkind?
ZUERST isst du die alten Socken und DANN bekommst du den leckeren Bikini!

When is it unlucky to see a black cat?

When you are a mouse!

Wörterverzeichnis

always [ˈɔːlweɪz] immer
angel [ˈeɪndʒəl] Engel
apple [ˈæpl] Apfel
astrologer [əˈstrɒlədʒə]
  Astrologe
awful [ˈɔːfʊl] furchtbar

bat [bæt] Fledermaus
beach [biːtʃ] Strand
because [bɪˈkɒz] weil
bell [bel] Klingel
be unlucky [bɪ ʌnˈlʌkɪ]
  Unglück bringen
big [bɪg] groß
blood [blʌd] Blut
bones [bəʊnz] Knochen
bookworm [ˈbʊkwɜːm]
  Bücherwurm
break [breɪk] Pause
breakfast [ˈbrekfəst]
  Frühstück

bright [braɪt] hell, klug,
  clever
broomstick [ˈbrʊmstɪk]
  Besenstiel

cake [keɪk] Kuchen
candle [ˈkændl] Kerze
can't [kɑːnt] kann nicht
cheese [tʃiːz] Käse
cheesy [ˈtʃiːzɪ] käsig
child [tʃaɪld] Kind
chimney [ˈtʃɪmnɪ]
  Schornstein
choir [ˈkwaɪə] Chor
Christmas [ˈkrɪsməs]
  Weihnachten
coffee [ˈkɒfɪ] Kaffee
coffin [ˈkɒfɪn] Sarg
cross [krɒs] kreuzen,
  überqueren

dance [dɑːns] tanzen
deliver [dɪ'lɪvə] abliefern
dinner ['dɪnə] Abendessen
dizzy ['dɪzɪ] schwindelig
down [daʊn] hinab, nach
   unten, ab
Do you speak …?
   [duː juː spiːk]
   Sprechen Sie …?
Dutch [dʌtʃ] holländisch

eat [iːt] essen
elephant ['elɪfənt] Elefant
every day ['evrɪ ˌdeɪ] jeden
   Tag
Excuse me! [ɪk'skjuːz mɪ]
   Entschuldigen Sie!

fast food [ˌfɑːst 'fuːd]
   Fastfood
feet [fiːt] Füße
fifty ['fɪftɪ] fünfzig
find [faɪnd] finden
fish and chip shop
   [fɪʃ ænd tʃɪp ʃɒp]
   Fisch-und-Pommes-
   Bude
flies [flaɪz] Fliegen
fly [flaɪ] fliegen, die Fliege
forty ['fɔːtɪ] vierzig
four [fɔː] vier
French [frentʃ] französisch
French fries [ˌfrentʃ 'fraɪz]
   Pommes frites
fridge [frɪdʒ] Kühlschrank
frogs [frɒgz] Frösche
fur coat ['fɜː kəʊt]
   Pelz(mantel)

G

get wet [get 'wet] nass
   werden
glasses ['glɑːsɪz] Brille
gooseberry ['gʊzbəri]
   Stachelbeere
go to the movies
   [gəʊ tʊ ðə 'muːvɪz] ins Kino
   gehen (amerik. Engl.)

H

hairy ['heəri] haarig
hate [heɪt] hassen
holes [həʊlz] Löcher

I

I'm fine. [aɪm 'faɪn] Es geht
   mir gut.
invisible [ɪn'vɪzəbl]
   unsichtbar

J/K

jaws [dʒɔːz] Rachen
joke [dʒəʊk] Witz

L

legs [legz] Beine
liar ['laɪə] Lügner(in)
lift [lɪft] Aufzug
live [lɪv] leben
lose [luːz] verlieren
lunch [lʌntʃ] Mittagessen

M

marry ['mæri] heiraten
memory ['meməri]
   Gedächtnis
merry ['meri] froh
mice [maɪs] Mäuse
micro- ['maɪkrəʊ] Mikro-
microwave ['maɪkrəweɪv]
   Mikrowelle

milk [mɪlk] Milch
moth [mɒθ] Motte
mouse [maʊs] Maus
movie ['muːvɪ] Film
much [mʌtʃ] viel
mummy ['mʌmɪ] Mumie,
  Mami

N

need [niːd] brauchen
no matter [nəʊ 'mætə] egal
  wie
nose [nəʊz] Nase

O

octopus ['ɒktəpəs] Krake
on holiday [ən 'hɒlədeɪ] im
  Urlaub

P/Q

patient ['peɪʃnt] Patient
pause [pɔːz] Pause
pen [pen] Füller,
  Kugelschreiber
pencil ['pensl] Bleistift
penguin ['peŋgwɪn] Pinguin
personally ['pɜːsnəlɪ]
  persönlich
pepper ['pepə] Pfeffer
plate [pleɪt] Teller
player ['pleɪə] Spieler(in)
polar bear [ˌpəʊlə'beə]
  Eisbär
pond [pɒnd] Teich
prove [pruːv] beweisen

R

rattle ['rætl] Rassel
rattlesnake ['rætlsneɪk]
  Klapperschlange
read [riːd] lesen

ring [rɪŋ] Klingel
roller-blades
    ['rəʊlə‿bleɪdz] Inliner

S

salt [sɔːlt] Salz
sandcastle ['sænd,kɑːsl]
    Sandburg
sandwich ['sænwɪdʒ]
    Sandwich
save [seɪv] retten
say [seɪ] sagen
screensaver ['skriːn,seɪvə]
    Bildschirmschoner
sea [siː] Meer
sea horse ['siːhɔːs]
    Seepferdchen
shall [ʃæl] soll
sick [sɪk] krank
silly ['sɪlɪ] dumm
sit [sɪt] sich setzen
sixteen [,sɪks'tiːn] sechzehn
skeleton ['skelɪtn] Skelett

slug [slʌg] Nacktschnecke
smell [smel] riechen
snail [sneɪl] Schnecke
snake [sneɪk] Schlange
sneeze [sniːz] niesen
snowball ['snəʊbɔːl]
    Schneeball
snowflake ['snəʊfleɪk]
    Schneeflocke
snowman ['snəʊmæn]
    Schneemann
snowmen ['snəʊmen]
    Schneemänner
soup [suːp] Suppe
space [speɪs] Weltraum
spider ['spaɪdə] Spinne
strawberry ['strɔːberɪ]
    Erdbeere
students ['stjuːdnts] Schüler
stupid ['stjuːpɪd] blöd,
    dumm
suddenly ['sʌdnlɪ] plötzlich
sun [sʌn] Sonne
sunglasses ['sʌn,glɑːsɪz]
    Sonnenbrille

T

test [test] Klassenarbeit,
   Blutprobe
tired ['taɪəd] müde
thumb [θʌm] Daumen

U

up [ʌp] hinauf, hoch, auf

V

vampire ['væmpaɪə] Vampir

W

waiter ['weɪtə] Ober, Kellner
wake up ['weɪkʌp]
   aufwachen
walk [wɔ:k] gehen
want [wɒnt] wollen
water ['wɔ:tə] Wasser

wave [weɪv] Welle
web [web] Netz
website ['websaɪt] Website
wet [wet] nass
wetter ['wetə] nasser
what [wɒt] was
What kind of ...?
   [wɒt kaɪnd əv]
   Was für ein/e/en ...?
where [weə] wohin
witch [wɪtʃ] Hexe
window ['wɪndəʊ] Fenster
woman ['wʊmən] Frau
worse [wɜ:s] schlimmer,
   schlechter
write [raɪt] schreiben

X / Y / Z

young [jʌŋ] jung
yummy ['jʌmɪ] lecker